2011 Edition

LUCION BOOKS

PO Box 20185

Roanoke, VA 20918

Table of Contents

Introduction

If you're not familiar with the "KNOW BRAINER'S", series, WELCOME. I'm a "KNOW BRAINER", and I know I'm not alone in this world. The purpose of this guide is to illustrate the importance of **"Priorities"** in every aspect of life.

What gives me the insight to write about **Priorities?** At my present age of 54, I'm lucky to be alive, for I have donated a lot of years to not following **Priorities**, and the ones I did follow leave a lot to be desired. So, through my many trials and tribulations I had numerous failures; some detrimental to my physical, mental, and spiritual well-being. So, by making so many mistakes, I can illuminate a path you can follow to help shape a healthy, wealthy, happy, and meaningful life full of success in all facets.

The first step in this guide is simple: some of the definitions of **"Priorities." Priorities** are defined as: (1) the state or quality of being earlier in time; (2) the right to precede others in order, rank, privilege, etc.; precedence; (3) the right to take precedence in obtaining certain supplies, services, facilities, etc.; (4) something given special attention; (5) highest or higher in importance, rank or privilege. It's true, **Priorities** cover all this, but it's so much more. By tearing the word down to its letters, I've made each letter into a word and devised an anagram to life. Not just any life, but a great life. In making it a **Priority** to finish this guide, it could be your life.

This easy to follow and understand "KNOW BRAINER'S" Guide will enlighten even the most ambiguous. What's so monumental about the "KNOW BRAINER'S" Guide is you don't have to go through all the grief I put myself through to finally see the light. After finishing the guide, pass it on. Sometimes, one's misfortunes can cause another's success. My misfortune leading to your success is one of the three **Priorities** I had in writing this Guide. The other two will follow upon completion.

Let's get started. The faster you finish the "KNOW BRAINER'S" Guide to **Priorities**, the easier your life will become; mentally, spiritually, and physically, and of course, financially. Remember, you have to pay the toll to Rock-n-Roll.

CHAPTER I

The Letter "P"

Well, we know that "P" is the first letter in Priorities-so with that, we'll form the word Persistently. It comes from the root word "persist." When defined (the word "persist"), it means: (1) to continue steadfastly or firmly in some state, purpose, or course of action in spite of opposition; (2) to last or endure tenaciously; (3) to be insistent in a statement, request or question; to stand firm permanently. I know you may be saying I could have gotten a dictionary and discovered that; which is true, but believe me, it will all fall together. Read on.

Have you ever been so down and out you didn't know where you next meal was coming from, much less your next drink or drug, or even a place to sleep? Been there-and what's so bad about it is, I did it by choice. I was not choosing good Priorities, or even being persistent at my bad ones. Let's just say, instead of going into my whole life's history, and what got me into that shape, which is a book in itself, I was a bum by choice, and nobody was forcing me.

I'd choose not to work, but to go and do just about anything I wanted whenever I wanted. Now I must say to go and do whatever you want, whenever, sounds OK, but without applying Priorities to be able to afford it left a lot to be desired. You've heard of being down and out in Beverly Hills? Well, I was down and out anywhere I went.

During my travels, to maintain a high-usually alcohol because everything else cost too much and stealing wasn't my thing-I panhandled for any amount that I could get to maintain that "buzz." My priority: "Stay high and get by!" Talk about a losing ticket, for some crazy reason back then it made some kind of sense. The thing is, I was a lousy panhandler. It caused me so much anguish to ask another person for spare change. The only time I could do it was when I was at least half drunk-and that was the catch 22- I needed money to get half drunk.

So through the pre-drunk haze I lived in, I would pick and choose my victims by the way they looked. Sometimes it worked, sometimes not, but it was always humiliating until I had that "buzz"-then it didn't matter anymore. Somehow I got by. Then one day I met this guy named Muskrat. Describing Muskrat would take pages-but to be brief, we usually referred to him as a sawed-off, half blind Texan, who was a little on the crude side. One day Muskrat said he'd be back in a few minutes with some money for some booze. He wasn't gone longer than a half an hour and he came back with about fifty dollars. I asked him whom he robbed. He said, "Nobody." I asked him whom he panhandled and he said, "Everybody." He told me that you have to be persistent. "Ask everyone. Don't give up if don't get the answer you want, ask someone else." Muskrat told me to persistently stick to it and you couldn't fail.

Day after day he'd go out and come back shortly with fifty, sixty dollars, or more. It never failed. All the tramps liked to have Muskrat around. He was a successful bum. I couldn't even follow my bad priority of being a bum with success because I couldn't be persistent. Even with the knowledge laid on me, by persistently asking everyone for money, my self esteem, or lack thereof, rendered me a failure at being a successful bum.

Whatever task at hand, whether it be physical, mental, or financial, your goal will be achieved if you persistently follow the course of action at hand. Lucky for me, I failed at being persistent and my career at being a bum was a failure. So by starting at the bottom and being an unsuccessful bum, I persistently changed into what I am now, the author of this guide. Whatever you're choosing, by persistently pursuing your Priorities, success will be inevitable. Hopefully your expectations are a lot higher than mine were back then, and with <u>persistently</u> applying your <u>Priorities,</u> yours will be accomplished.

CHAPTER 2

The Letter "R"

The second letter in <u>Priorities</u> is R; and we'll use the word "<u>Resolving.</u>" <u>Resolving</u> comes from the root word "resolve." I'm going to lay out a few definitions for you, but as you'll see, there's so much more. Some definitions of resolve are: (1) to come to definite earnest decision; (2) to separate into constituent or elemental parts, break up, cause to disintegrate; (3) to convert or transform by any process; (4) to reduce by mental analysis; (5) to determine or state formally in a vote or resolution; (6) to deal with a question, a matter of uncertainty, settle, solve; (7) to clear away or dispel doubts, fears, etc.; (8) to come to a determination, make up one's mind; (9) firmness of purpose or intent; and (10) analyze, unfold, unravel, decipher, dissipate, clear, or rid. The list goes on and on, but I think any "Know Brainer" should have gotten the gist of it by now. With the "ing" ending added to resolve, it means to be continually doing so.

So when mapping out your <u>Priorities</u>, you have to be <u>resolving</u> whatever, whoever, whenever, however, and why ever, and all the other "evers" that come across your path. If you're fat and you want to lose weight, you've got to eat less and more nutritiously, and work out. If that's your problem, you'll lose weight if you're <u>persistently</u> (remember that word) <u>resolving</u> the problem. Any problem you face, if you break it down to its simplest form, then deal with it, any "Know Brainer" can do it.

In math for instance, the quality of the model depends on the quality of its assumptions; the quality of the answer depends on the quality of the question. The answer, in fact, becomes inevitable once the questions stated properly. It works in math, in can work in life. In "Know Brainer" terms: Ask the question based on quality assumptions and you're going to get the answer. Do you want to be rich; simple question? With whatever endeavor you have in mind, <u>persistently</u> <u>resolving</u> all the assumptions with quality will give you the answer: Yes. When you come to the determination of what you want in life, all you have to do is set your course of action. It starts with your <u>Priorities</u>.

When I was twelve, I heard a song, "I can't get no satisfaction." The Rolling Stones hit the nail right on the head for me. I was unsatisfied with my life. I didn't have everything I wanted—I guess no kid ever does, except those born with a silver spoon. But it wasn't all about money. So for a couple of years, I did what a lot of kids do: listened to music, played sports, tried to stay out of trouble, and started to really be attracted to the opposite sex.

Then with all the un-satisfaction I had came the remedies for my pain: alcohol, then drugs. It felt great! I was almost cured; at least I thought I was. Then around fourteen years old, it happened: my childhood sweet heart said "yes," and I was a man— at least I thought I was.

I loved Rock-n-Roll music from jump-street, and the way Rock-Stars got the women, money, drugs, and alcohol. There was no question; I wanted to be a Rock-Star. I made it a priority. With that being my priority, I tried to get all the women, drink all the liquor, do all the dope, and get all the money I could.

Now wanting to be a Rock-Star is fine for one's personal priority. My problem was I wasn't resolving my priority by doing the work to become a Rock-Star. I tried to get all the girls I could, and cheated on my girlfriend, which was wrong and brought on unnecessary grief to her and the other girls involved. I drank and did drugs a lot. To allow myself access to the both, I was selling drugs. Now I was more-or-less living the life of a Rock-Star. Only problem was, I wasn't a rock star. I didn't donate my time to learn the guitar or even learn the lyrics to the songs. I never even tried to get in a band, or do any of the work involved. My priority was fine. My method of resolving the obstacles, that stopped me from achieving. It was all wrong.

So when you set your sights on whatever goal you have in mind and make it one of your Priorities. You have to be persistently resolving the obstacles in your path to make it possible without causing unnecessary pain for all involved. You have to dispel any doubts and fears. You have to achieve your goals, resolving only success as an outcome. In the meantime, bring joy to yourself and all involved along the journey. Again, maybe my lack of resolving Priorities in the past will add to your insight in resolving yours in the future. In the long run, if that's true, I'm resolving one of mine—it's a win, win situation. By persistently resolving your Priorities, success is inevitable.

CHAPTER 3

The Letter "I"

The next letter in <u>Priorities</u> is "I;" and as we build our anagram, we'll use the "I" to draw your "<u>interest</u>." Some of the common definitions of the word interest" are as follows: (1) the feeling or a person whose attention, concern or curiosity is particularly engaged by something; (2) power of exciting such concern, involvement; (3) a business cause of the like in which a person has a share, concern, or responsibility; (4) a share, right or title in the ownership of a property; (5) the state of being affected by something in respect to advantage; and (6) benefit, advantage, to have one's own <u>interest</u> in mind.

In life, your <u>interest</u> may lead you down a wide variety of paths. Some good, some bad; you don't know which one until it evolves into what it will become. When using your <u>Priorities</u> wisely, your <u>interest</u>s play a major role in health, happiness and financial well-being: leading to a life with peace of mind.

Why approach any part of life if you don't have the <u>interest</u> in it. Everybody's got to do some kind of work in this old world to survive—unless you were born rich. Even then, you still have to do something of <u>interest</u>. A wise man once said, "It is a great joy to love the work you do; and probably dangerous not to." Being the "Know Brainer" I am, it took me a long <u>time</u> to understand that saying, much less, to come into agreement with in. I have probably had over a hundred different jobs in my life, in a vast variety.

One <u>time</u> in life, I got this job as a carpenter's helper, building a laboratory for a tobacco manufacturing company. I love building things with my hands, but this was form carpentry; a lot a concrete work and tying steel. Anyway, I had no <u>interest</u> in it. Every day, I'd get up and dread the idea of another day of it. The only release I found is when the 5:00 whistle blew. <u>Believe me. I wasn't alone</u>. A whole caravan of us would head down to one of the local watering holes to drink away the blues. Every night, I'd try to drink myself into some kind of contentment, and usually succeed. The next morning, the alarm would go off and, maybe after three or four hours of drunken sleep, I'd get up and go do it again. Every morning the same dread would jump right up into my face. All day long I'd go through the paces, hating being there, but I had to work. My solution: when I got off in the afternoon, I'd hit the bottle. Then, I could deal with my life and my job.

So my bright idea was to hit the bottle in the morning—have a drink before work. That led me to mixing liquor in my coffee thermos to maintain throughout the day. Needless to say, what an asshole I was for not only endangering my life, but also the lives of those around me. Thankfully, no one ever suffered any physical injury from my abuse of alcohol at work. But verbally, I probably abused quite a few people.

The old term "loose lips sink ships," well I was a happy sailor dancing on a sinking ship. I'd quit one job after another for lack of interest—and the only thing of interest came out of a bottle. The dangerousness of the old saying came into play. So, not having interest in work led me into another interest, "alcohol." That only made things worse.

Set your Priorities, with all its definitions, for the failure to do so usually leads to a downfall of some nature. The "Know Brainer" way, I did the work and had the downfalls—hopefully, saving you some grief.

In health, if you don't take an interest in it, you probably won't last too long. If there is such a thing as luck, I'm lucky I'm here, because my health was the last thing I ever use to have an interest in. The old saying "you are what you eat," a cliché, but a good one. If you are young or old, it's never too late to take an interest in your health. When you get my age and finally had an awakening, your clock has less <u>time</u> left on it.

When I was a kid, my Mom would always try her best to get me to eat right—bless her heart—but my only <u>interest</u> was in candy and soda pop. Believe me, I was one wired-up kid with rotten teeth. Hopefully, if you're young, you'll take my advice. And if you're old, it's never too late; pass it on. Be good to yourself. Take an <u>interest</u> in your health. Good food, good exercise, good long life—easy math.

If happiness is what you're <u>interested</u> in, do some more math. If you're doing a job that makes your life <u>interest</u>ing, if you are eating right and keeping your body physically fit, if you make a good living, are physically sound and you share a positive outlook with someone else you are sexually attracted to and share similar <u>interest</u>, it will leave little <u>time</u> in life for anything but happiness. Another win-win situation! You do the math if you have the "<u>interest</u>."

CHAPTER 4

The letter "O"

As the word "Priorities" progresses, so do we—to the next letter, "O." With the letter "0," we'll use the word "orchestrating." A couple of definitions to refresh your memory: (1) to compose or arrange (music) for performance by an orchestra; and (2) to arrange or manipulate, by means of clever or through planning or maneuvering.

In our first definition, of orchestrating, I believe in almost everyone that music of some form or style brings about some form of emotion. I like most categories of music when it's put together right. The rewards are usually vast and satisfying. Then there's that high note when, right at the crescendo, the note comes out flat or off key. What a bummer. And it's all due to not orchestrating properly. If the musician would have arranged his music with a note he could have manipulated, it would be all good. By not hitting it, both our ears and his pride have to suffer—such is life.

Orchestrating through life, as in music, we must arrange things properly and in perspective in all areas. We must manipulate the pieces of the puzzle to make it fit. Once again, the 'Know Brainer" way, I was Orchestrating through life, but I couldn't hit that 'high note" on more than one occasion. I would set my Priorities on one thing, and by not orchestrating all the instruments together, I achieved *all but perfect harmony*.

Early in my life, I fell victim to the judicial system, ending up in the Department of Corrections system. I was arrested for distribution of marijuana—a small amount, but still another bad choice of Priorities and execution. This led to a weary and long progression down and through the legal machine. I'm not going to dwell on the how's or why's in this guide as to my circumstances, but the effects. After a brief stay in the Virginia Department of Corrections, I was released on probation and a suspended sentence. I was, to say the least, displeased with the system, my charges, the men and circumstances in prison, and the world in general. Now maybe if I'd had a guide like this when I was younger, I wouldn't have had a lot of my misadventures and failed Priorities in life. Then by the same token, in the end, my new Priorities, because of my past downfalls and what I learned from them, will be answered and many a life my benefit.

Upon release, I tried to get a job, but to my surprise, a young man with a rap sheet for drugs didn't meet many an employer's ideal criteria. Then I tried another direction in my orchestrating of some kind of career, I lied. Another bad choice, as not only do lies gain in size, like a snowball rolling down a snow- covered hill, but they usually lead that snow ball right to the gates of hell. As we know, snow and fire don't mix well.

I went to one job interview I was actually interested in. The job involved operating a small crane and repairing large engines for excavating equipment. The boss man liked me at the interview and called me back. They gave me a mechanical aptitude test to see if I'd work out, and I passed it with flying colors. Then the boss man hit me with the old cliché, if there are no skeletons in your closet, you've got the job." The lie caught up with me and I was turned down because of it. I 'm not going into the correctness of his decision to pass on me for having a felony record, but I did lie about it and it caught up with me, and it would again and again in my life. The outcome of this made me even more pissed off at the system. I was fed up with everyone and just about everything.

I changed my Priorities and got back in school on a prison rehabilitation grant, and actually used the system to my benefit. I knew what I wanted to do. I wanted to be a forest ranger. That way I could be as far away from everything and everybody, and still make a good living. As a priority, being a forest ranger is fine, but my orchestrating of my priority fell far short of hitting the high note.

Going to college was a big change from what I just experienced. It was just a community college, but being around a lot of kids around my age with the normal things on their minds, compared to being around a lot of large men with anything but what was normal on their minds, was definitely a pleasant change. I felt a little strange at times, but I was never much at school anyway.

In order to become a park ranger I needed a degree in biology to start off with. So that's what I took, and all the other necessary classes. I was struggling, for I couldn't see why I needed to know about one celled organisms to become a park ranger. I went to see my counselor to talk about it and that's when my "high note" came out totally flat. In orchestrating my career move I hadn't done much research. My counselor informed me to work for the Forestry Department to be a forest ranger I couldn't have a felony on my record. Talk about that flat note. I'd been busting my butt for the last couple of months trying to achieve something I couldn't, just because of my past. What a waste. Now I was even more sick and tired of the system and the world. So many more misadventures followed. Sometimes, you are your own worst enemy.

If I'd been <u>orchestrating</u> through life with my instruments in tune, maybe I would have been able to hit that "high note;" but not back then. Nothing sounds any better than a great orchestra, or a life that plays out like a sweet love song. So, while you're <u>orchestrating</u> through life, try to keep your instruments in tune and sing on key.

CHAPTER 5

The letter "R"

In the spelling of Priorities we're up to the letter "R;" and what's better than some rewards. We'll touch of a few of the definitions to get you going in the right direction to receive yours, such as: (1) a sum of money offered for the detection or capture of a criminal, the recovery of lost or stolen property; (2) something given or received in return or recompense for service, merit, achievement; (3) to recompense or requite; and (4) pay, remuneration, requital, bounty, premium, bonus, prize, etc. I will leave the definitions with this thought, "Virtue is its own reward."

Your rewards should be in all phases of your life if you use your Priorities correctly. That's just what this guide is all about: getting you from the beginning of Priorities to the end, resulting in rewards.

On a dark and rainy day, I rolled off my bunk in a prison cell in a mental health unit and stood on a bum ankle that had been screwed-up in an operation a year previously. Well, that sounds like enough to qualify me as a real blues-man, doesn't it? But, it gets worse. I was there for something that I didn't do, and my remedy was food. I was a little on the fat side. I was trying to eat away the blues, but it only made it worse. I said to myself, "What has happened to me?" I still say that to myself at <u>times</u>, but the answer is totally different now.

I dropped to the floor and tried to do twenty-five push-ups. I barely cranked out ten. I started right at that point to set about a change in myself—physically, mentally, and spiritually. I started with the physical part. I made it one of my <u>Priorities</u> and changes happened. (If you're <u>interested</u> in my physical metamorphosis, or how you can do the same, there is another "Know Brainer's" guide to physical fitness out there with all the "whys" and "hows.") The change was in progress and I set a <u>time</u> table for goals, and achieved them, and still continue to, for change is constant. With a healthy body, guess what, the minds follows.

As I got healthier, I came out of the fog I was in. As much as I exercised my body, my mind also cried out for exercise. I feed my body good fuel, or the best I had access to. I also started feeding my mind, and constantly still do. What used to seem like a pain became a passion. I used to wake up in the morning and had to really press my willpower to the limit to start working out. Then it happened. The workout paid off with <u>rewards</u>: a new weight; muscle tone; strength and a zest for life.

I started reading things I found of <u>interest</u>. Again, hard at first, it was a real pain. Then it happened. I didn't have enough time to read all I wanted and I became <u>interest</u>ed in almost everything. More <u>rewards</u>—pain to passion.

The body started it off, next came the mind, and then the spirituality kicked in. Virtue is its own reward. Whatever your problems are, if you set your <u>Priorities</u> in gear, <u>rewards</u> are the outcome. If you are physically down-trodden, set your <u>Priorities</u> and follow them. When you look into the mirror and you like what you see, that's a just reward. If financial gain is one of your goals, follow your <u>Priorities</u>. Use them correctly and a fat bank account will be rewarded. With a healthy body and mind, and a fat bank account, and having a passion in exchange for pain, the spirit will follow suit. You'll be able to say, "Virtue is its own reward;" and know what you're talking about. How's that for a reward.

CHAPTER 6

The letter 'I"

As our spelling of <u>Priorities</u> goes on, we run across another letter: "I." This <u>time</u> we'll ask you to do a little "<u>Investing</u>." The root word is "invest." Here are a few of the definitions to get us started: (1) to put money to use by purchase or expenditure in something offering potential profitable returns as <u>interest</u>, income, or appreciation in value; (2) to use, give, or devote <u>time</u>, talent, etc.; (3) to furnish with power, authority, rank, etc.; and (4) to infuse or belong to, as a quality or characteristic. There are plenty more, but this is enough to be <u>Investing</u> for our requirements.

In everything we do in life we have to invest either physically, mentally, or spiritually to receive some form of reaction; whether it is good or bad. Any "Know Brainer" ought to be able to figure that out. A good investment usually turns into a good reward; and a bad investment usually a bad outcome. I'm not saying you can't have a bad experience and turn it into a favorable outcome. Me, as example, all my bad investments caused me lots of pain, but the experiences, hopefully, allowed me to lead you into not wasting your <u>time</u> as I did. That is what this guide is all about: setting your <u>Priorities</u>

into motion and Investing the right ingredients to end up with a just reward.

If in finance you make a wise investment, you will obtain a profitable dividend. In your health, if you invest the time to work out properly and eat nutritiously, you'll receive the reward of a physically fit body. Mentally, what and how much you feed the mind will result in the knowledge you obtain. Spiritually, you'll be able to process your knowledge you've obtained—the good and the bad, for it comes in both flavors—in a virtuous matter. Again, virtue is its own reward. As this guide goes on and you're Investing your time, the math should become easier to understand. The Investing of your time on the math will lead to many benefits—a win-win situation.

Some people are Investing their time in chasing rainbows to get to the pot of gold at the end; when, if they were Investing wisely, they would see that the colors are the same from the beginning to the end. There's gold at both ends and all the way through. That's what Investing in your Priorities is all about. How you invest from the beginning to the end.

Once upon a time, there were three characters sitting in a vacant lot, a buzzard, a turtle, and a rabbit. They had just each received a third in an inheritance. The first thing they did with their newly obtained money was to go out and bought a case of cheap, rot gut wine; and, were about half way through it, when they figured out an investment for the rest of their money. They noticed that all around them, almost every house had a garden. The Buzzard, with a twinkle in his eye, said, "I've got it. Everyone in this county has a garden. A couple of counties away, everyone raises livestock." The Turtle and the rabbit said, "So what." The Buzzard said, "Everyone with a garden needs fertilizer; and a couple of counties away, everyone raises livestock.

The Buzzard said, "Since everyone with a garden need fertilizer, and a couple of counties away, everyone raises livestock (a Know Brainer"), we'll go into the manure business. We'll buy it cheap a couple of counties away, bring it over to this vacant lot, and sell it for a profit to all the people with gardens." "They've got to have fertilizer," he said. So it all sounded like a wise investment.

The Turtle looked at the Buzzard and said, "Mr. Buzzard, since you can fly real fast, you fly over and pick up the manure." The Buzzard said, "Yes, I can fly, but I can't carry that much." Then the Buzzard said, "Turtle, you're strong, so why don't you get the manure." The Turtle said, I am strong, but you know how slow we turtles are. It would take forever." Then, in unison, the Buzzard and the Turtle said, "Mr. Rabbit, you're strong and fast. You could hop on over real fast and carry a good sized load." So the Rabbit said, "O.K., you guys buy the vacant lot for our business and I'll take the rest of the money on the manure run.

So the rabbit hops into the sunset. The Rabbit returns in a couple of weeks with the manure, and on the vacant lot, there's a mansion. The Rabbit un-straps himself from the cart of manure and walks up to the door. "Knock, knock, knock." A very dignified butler with a distinguished voice answers the door and says, "Yes? May I help you?" The Rabbit asks, "Where's Mr. Buzzard" The butler replied, "Mr. Buzz-a-r-d is out in the ya-r-d." Then the Rabbit asked, "Where's Mr. Turtle? The butler replied, "Mr. Turt-e-l-l is down by the we-l-l." So then the Rabbit said, "You go tell Mr. Buzz-a-r-d, whose out in the ya-r-d, and Mr. Turt-e-l-l, whose down by the we-l-l, that Mr. Rab-b-i-t is back with the *sh-i-t.*"

Now I don't know how these three made out in their Investing, but they stepped right in it. By you Investing the time to read of their journey, maybe a grin came to the corner of your mouth; which, hopefully, goes to show you that Investing wisely is the way to go, but you must enjoy the journey. So, like the rainbow and its colors, you'll

share in the Gold from beginning to end by
<u>Investing</u> all the way through.

CHAPTER 7

The letter "I"

If you don't get anything else out of this guide, you'll definitely know the spelling of Priorities. Hopefully, you'll get so much more— that's on you. The next letter is "T;" and just in time, for "time" is our word. So, let's get started, for as the saying goes, "You can't make up for lost time." I'm only going to give you a few definitions—for time's sake—for most dictionaries get carried away with time. Time is defined as: (1) the system of those sequential relations that any event has to any other as past, present, or future; indefinite and continuous duration regarded as that in which events succeed one another; (2) duration regarded as belonging to the present life as distinct from the life to come or from eternity: finite duration; (3) a system or method of measuring or reckoning the passage of time; (4) a limited period or interval; (5) a particular period considered as distinct from other periods; (6) a period with reference to personal experience of a specific kind; (7) a particular part of the year, month, day, etc.; and (8) a term of enforced duty or imprisonment.

I'm going to stop on that one because it sort of hits home. As I'm writing this guide, I'm doing time; incarcerated. I'm not going into the "whys" or "what-fors," but as I said earlier, I've made many mistakes. Hopefully, the time, I've done—there's been plenty of it-is not a waste: for I truly hope this guide helps many use their time and Priorities better than I did, the "Know Brainer" way.

There are so many clichés associated with time I could throw at you that make a world of sense. I'll try not to but sometimes they just fit. Time is on your side. It doesn't matter whether its twenty years or twenty minutes—it's all about your use of it. During my younger days, I truly didn't think that I would live to see thirty; and that people over thirty couldn't be trusted. Those were some wasted days. Then I hit thirty, and everything still seemed the same. Then I heard when you hit forty, you're over the hill. I don't even hardy remember climbing up the hill. But I guess I must have, for I'm still here. Then at fifty, you're older than the hills. What I'm getting at is the number doesn't mean anything; you're as young as you feel, and you're also as old as you feel. It's all in your use of the time you do have on this Earth.

There's no making up for lost time. Now is what you're thinking of then, and then is what you're thinking of now. Sounds kind of like some Chinese philosophy or something. But if that's the way you look at it, all you're doing is going in circles, daydreaming— lost time. Don't get stuck in the circle. Use the wisdom of the past in dealing with the present, in the perception of a more prolific future. In Priorities, you start at the beginning and you don't end up till the lights go out. It's all about the use of time—time well spent. If you are investing time and you follow your Priorities and use them as illustrated in this guide, rewards are sure to come in time.

You can't rush time. When you set your Priorities, there's going to be some sort of time lime. If you're trying to lose weight and you starve yourself and go crazy working out, you'll probably end up sick and injured. You've got to be realistic in your assessment of a time line. Rome wasn't built in a day. There's one of those clichés—but how true. If you take your time dieting nutritiously, and set a workout schedule, with a time table you can handle without resulting in injury, you'll be well on your way to the rewards you desire.

A baby's got to crawl before it walks. In using time wisely, so do you. Set your Priorities in steps. If it's a five-step plan, don't rush it and jump from two to five. It may result in injury, physically, mentally, or financially. It's all about your management of time.

People have asked me what it's like being in prison. After timely deliberation—to be brief—my answer is, "You're in prison only in the physical state; but it's like one long day that never ends until you get out." Again, it's all about how you spent that one long day. The monotony of prison life is brain-numbing—the same every day. It's all about waiting. You wait, literally, for everything. Again, it's about how you use the waiting time. There can be a whole world of things to do while waiting for one physical time span. I have manipulated my waiting time into a constant change physically, mentally, and spiritually, as I spoke about earlier in this guide. Any waiting time I have, I'll use it exercising some physical body part, or I'll be reading and studying, expanding my mind, and both, in turn, leading to some spirituality and peace of mind. The 'Know Brainer' way, turn a negative into a positive in your use of time.

   It's like when a writer finds his voice, or an artist freezes time in a still-life, or a seeker sees the light. In time, with time on your side, not trying to make up for lost time, time well spent, and not rushing time, taking one step at a time and not becoming a prisoner of time, you'll find your voice, paint a masterpiece, and surely see the light. Now's the time.

CHAPTER 8

The letter "I"

In your spelling of <u>Priorities</u>, our next letter is another "I." We've discussed "<u>interest</u>," and "<u>Investing</u>." Now we're going to use the letter "I" in "<u>integrity</u>." To get us started, again, we'll start with a few definitions: (1) adherence to moral and ethical principles, soundness of moral character, honesty; (2) the state of being whole, entire, or undiminished; and (3) a sound, unimpaired, or perfect condition.

When you set your <u>Priorities</u>, if you use <u>integrity</u>, you'll not only receive physical, mental, and financial <u>rewards</u>, but also spiritual <u>rewards</u>. Not only will your <u>Priorities</u> be self-gratifying, but they will have the "domino-effect," and those around you will also receive great satisfaction. Remember, virtue is its own reward. The more <u>integrity</u> you use, the stronger the saying stands.

I explained earlier how one lie will roll into the next; like a snowball rolling to the Gates of Hell. So why not be a ""Know Brainer"?" Don't hurt yourself. Be Honest.

In my prison experience, just as in life, I've met many a man. I've heard men swear to stories taller than the Sears' Tower. In my earlier days, I told a few, thinking it would help me in the pursuit of my <u>Priorities</u>. In the long run, it's just a recipe for failure. You can't live a lie, unless you want nothing. A lie is based on falseness or nothing real. So all you're going to end up with by <u>investing</u> nothing is nothing. Easy math—be good to yourself, use the "Know Brainer" way, and tell the truth. If you don't even believe yourself, why do you think that somebody else would believe you? It's all about <u>integrity</u>.

If you're building a house, and you leave out a few of the floor joists to save money, sooner or later, probably sooner, the floor is going to cave in. It's just the same with your <u>Priorities</u> in life. If they're not solid, your life will cave in. I know, for mine has caved in so many <u>times</u>, the bottom has looked like up. Again, be good to yourself. Use good strong wood in building your <u>Priorities</u> and use it all. Don't leave any out, or in the end, it will collapse. "Start square, stay square," works in building <u>success</u>ful buildings and it works in life. It's all about <u>integrity</u>.

Once upon a <u>time</u> in my life, the way I was gaining my ill-gotten-gains was by selling what we called "86 `ers." Now all of this is totally about bad <u>Priorities</u>, the use of them, and the effect. What the 86'ers were or these little pills you could buy at an organic mechanic shop (health food store). The pills were supposedly organic antihistamines. But actually, they didn't do anything to or for you. However, they looked like micro-dots (LSD). It's bad enough selling drugs, I'd already did <u>time</u> for that. So, in my spaced out brain, I wasn't breaking the law, for it wasn't real LSD.

In my travels on this occasion, I was passing through Rockford, Illinois. I went into a biker bar to have a drink. I had enough money just to get the buzz started, but I wouldn't leave it unfinished. So I broke the 86'ers out and started selling them for $3.00 a piece, or two for $5.00. I don't know if you've ever been in a biker bar with a gang of half-drunk bikers, and start selling them LSD. That's pretty dangerous. Only thing worse is selling them LSD —you guessed it— that isn't real. There I was. Now you probably can see why I didn't think I'd live to see thirty.

I was a king pin for a while. Everyone was anticipating the dope to kick in at any <u>time</u>. Trouble being, this <u>time,</u> <u>time</u> wasn't on my side, for I knew I had to ***beat feet*** before these guys saw that they had been beat. To make a long story short, I made it as far as the parking lot in my escape attempt. When I came to, my boots were gone, my leather coat, my goose down sleeping bag, all my worldly possessions, except my pants. Thank God! They did leave me with about thirty to thirty-five assorted bruises in assorted places, a broken nose, and freezing cold. Believe it or not, I've been in worse positions. But, I haven't been back to Rockford since; and really don't have any plans to head back that way.

Point being, my whole scam had no integrity. I didn't have a solid foundation. Everything was based on a lie. You can see how it ended up. My Priorities were all wrong from the start. Hopefully, my past pain will aid in your much better use of your integrity in following your Priorities.

So, start square and stay square. Use all your tools with integrity in your pursuit of Priorities and rewards are sure to follow.

CHAPTER 9

The letter "E"

We've getting toward the end of the spelling of <u>Priorities</u>. With our next letter, "E," what better <u>time</u> to use the word "<u>Equaling</u>," to make it all balance out. The root of the word being "equal," let's look up a few definitions, such as: (1) as great as, the same as; (2) like or alike in quantity, degree, value, etc.., of the same rank, ability, merit, etc.; (3) evenly proportioned or balanced; (4) uniform in operation or effect; (5) adequate or sufficient in quantity or degree; (6) having adequate powers, ability or means; and (7) level as a plain. In the adding of the ing to equal, it puts the word in continuous use.

Everything we've discussed previously in this guide has to be equaled out. By <u>Equaling</u> them properly, the <u>rewards</u> you desire will be achieved. Any "Know Brainer" knows that one action causes a re-action. What we're concerned with, in the word "<u>Equaling</u>," is doing just that, <u>Equaling</u> the actions and re-actions out, so they end up as a beneficial reward to following our <u>Priorities</u>.

If, in following your <u>Priorities</u>, your main priority is to get rich, there's nothing wrong with that. But if it kills you—why? You've got to look at the whole picture in your <u>Priorities</u>—how to be healthy, wealthy, happy, and have peace of mind. That's what this guide is all about: tearing it apart and putting it back together; whether it's the word or your life. Equaling all aspects of your life out, one part will be beneficial to the other parts, and vice-a-versa.

There once was this guy I knew and he went through life not Equaling out the actions and re-actions. He wanted health, happiness, wealth, and peace of mind; the same things most people desire. He didn't want to invest time properly, wanting instant gratification. Always putting the cart in front of the horse. Seeking the rewards without resolving the task at hand. Trying to play the song before the guitar was in tune. Orchestrating without the music in key. He would jump form one way of life to another without persistently following any Priorities to make it a success. He had no integrity, not caring who, or what he harmed to get what he wanted. Have you ever met anyone that would fall into such a category?

Like I said, I did. He was the guy who looked back at me when I looked in the mirror. I don't know if anyone else looks in the mirror and sees that reflection—I sincerely hope not. But if you see him or her, it's never too late to change. If you just see a part of that reflection, it's also wise to change that reflection early before the wear and tear sets in. That's the whole idea behind this guide: using your Priorities to gain rewards every time you look in the mirror, to obtain health, wealth, happiness, and peace of mind and not hurt anyone in the process; especially not yourself. So, in Equaling out your life, put it on the scale and make sure it's balanced correctly.

CHAPTER 10

The Letter "S"

Well, the last letter in Priorities is "S;" and with the letter "S" we'll use "Success"—and what better way could we end. Success is what we're always in pursuit of in one way or another. Let's see what the dictionary has to say about success: (1) the favorable or prosperous termination of attempts or endeavors; (2) the attainment of wealth, position, honor, or the like; (3) a successful performance or achievement; (4) outcome; and (5) a desired end.

That's what most people are after, a desired end. But, that's just part of it. What you want is not just the destination to be desirable, but the whole journey. In using Priorities the way I laid it out in the Guide, your whole trip can be rewarding from beginning to end. It's all on you. Any "Know Brainer" can do it. There's really no secret to any of this. All we're talking about is words we've all heard millions of times before—nothing new—but it's all about how they are arranged.

Now you have it all spelled out. The "quality," the spelling of "Priorities," depends on the "quality" of the assumptions—the letters that make it up—i.e., the "quality" of the question: "Will I succeed?" Then the answer in fact becomes inevitable once the question is stated properly.

Success is the outcome by using all fundamentals of the letters we used as our words in the spelling of Priorities we asked the questions properly.

You do the math. You're the one you'll see when you look in the mirror. If you use your knowledge in this Guide, you should see a reflection of success.

CHAPTER 11

"What's that spell?"

We all know by now it spells <u>Priorities</u>. Now, let's combine the words we matched-up with the letters in the spelling of <u>Priorities</u>, and this is what we get. <u>Priorities</u> is <u>persistently</u> <u>resolving</u> <u>interest</u>(s), <u>orchestrating</u> <u>rewards</u>, <u>Investing</u> <u>time</u>, <u>integrity</u>, <u>Equaling</u> <u>success</u>. Read over that sentence a few <u>times</u> and you don't even have to do the math—it does it for you. All you have to do is follow it from beginning to end in <u>success</u>. Be good to yourself. Any "Know Brainer" can do it.

Have you ever asked anyone about the "glass of water" to see whether they're an optimist or pessimist. When in fact, what if they say they're neither—they're equal. Every action does have a reaction. So if you ever seem like you're up against the wall by some negative action, try a positive re-action. Maybe you'll find out that 50% of the <u>time</u>, they'll equal out. It works if you use the right recipe; and I gave you that in the spelling of <u>Priorities</u>. <u>Priorities</u> is <u>persistently</u> <u>resolving</u> <u>interest</u>(s), <u>orchestrating</u> <u>rewards</u>, <u>Investing</u> <u>time</u>, <u>integrity</u>, <u>Equaling</u> <u>success</u>.

If you've got the idea through reading this guide that I've had my back against the wall more than once, you really don't even know the half of it.

Now, I let what use to be the pains become a passion. Instead of letting things work against you, let them work for you. A negative becomes a positive. Make the most of every bad situation and turn it around. Me being the Know Brainer," I am ended up in so many negative situations by not knowing my Priorities, or how to chose, use or follow them.

The Know Brainer" way: let someone else do the road work for you. That's me. Now you can save a lot of time and grief by just using one sentence. Persistently resolving interest(s), orchestrating rewards, Investing time integrity, Equaling success—"Priorities."

You can take every word that we used in the sentence and know that it's "All Good." When you put them together, they speak for themselves. So, in your search for the answers, just ask the right questions and your Priorities will lead you through a life of Health, Wealth, Happiness, and Peace of Mind from beginning to end.

CHAPTER 12

"My Three Priorities in Writing This Guide."

My first priority was to put my idea on paper and finish it. When I started writing, I was trying to write for the young and old, female, male, black, white, red, yellow and all mixes of the above, and both the rich and poor. In other words: everyone. I wanted to get in where I fit in.

I carried the thoughts of the word Priorities in my mind for about a year. I looked back on how many bad Priorities I followed, and how I failed at my good ones. So, with all the time I had to think, I tried to formulate a system so my next priority would lead to success in whatever I chose. Then, I tried to get it all on paper. Many times, I thought I wrote myself into a corner. I did learn about what writer's call "writer's block." I guess it comes with the territory. I have read many a "self-help" and "how-to" books, and not to be disrespectful to the authors, but a lot of them were a little drawn out. I tried to be brief and get to the point—get it over with and let you get on to the pursuit of—what else—your Priorities. I finished this Guide; and with it, one of my Priorities was fulfilled.

My second priority in finishing this Guide was to sincerely help any and all who read it to save time and misfortunes in the pursuit of their

Priorities. To help them fulfill them and be happy from the beginning to the end. Through my hardships in life, which were brought on by no one else but me, maybe the insight will help you. I know I've done a lot of damage in my life to others and myself—for this I am truly sorry. I can't turn back the hands of or make up for lost <u>time</u>. But the <u>time</u> I have left, I can use wisely. In writing this guide, hopefully helping anyone who reads it to be rewarded with a healthy, wealthy, happy life filled with peace of mind, I will be rewarded with my own peace of mind. Another old saying, "What comes around, goes around."

My third priority in writing this Guide is to make a bunch of money while following my <u>Priorities</u>. If you bought this Guide, it helped. "Thank you very much." I hope you prosper from it in all aspects. If you didn't buy it and someone turned you on to it, that's cool too. If you got it by illegal or immoral methods, the only thing I have to say is this: "You better change your <u>Priorities</u> for if you don't, they have a place for you. And believe you me; it leaves a lot to be desired."

Be good to yourself.

W.C. Lucion

I was locked up when I wrote this book. Since then my life has changed in many ways all for the good, I work hard at the things I do but as the old saying goes if you love your work you never work a day in your life. I have found happiness and peace of mind in every aspect of life. The reason being I not only wrote this book but I live it. Upon reading it I hope you are also blessed.

If interested in giving me your feedback. Contact:

William Charles Lucion

P O. Box 20185

Roanoke, Virginia. 24018

www.ingramcontent.com/pod-product-compliance
Lightning Source LLC
Chambersburg PA
CBHW071025040426
42443CB00007B/935